aFresh Start

a 30-day follow-through on your commitment to **Christ**

Scott Larson

Group

Loveland, Colorado

Group's R.E.A.L. Guarantee to you:

This Group resource incorporates our R.E.A.L. approach to ministry—one that encourages long-term retention and life transformation. It's ministry that's:

Relational
Because learner-to-learner interaction enhances learning and builds Christian friendships.

Experiential
Because what learners experience through discussion and action sticks with them up to 9 times longer than what they simply hear or read.

Applicable
Because the aim of Christian education is to equip learners to be both hearers and doers of God's Word.

Learner-based
Because learners understand and retain more when the learning process takes into consideration how they learn best.

A Fresh Start
A 30-Day Follow-Through on Your Commitment to Christ
Copyright © 2003 Scott Larson

Visit our Web site: **www.group.com**
Visit Scott's ministry Web site: **www.straightahead.org**

Credits
Development Editor: Amy Simpson
Editor: Paul Woods
Chief Creative Officer: Joani Schultz
Assistant Editor: Alison Imbriaco
Art Director: Kari K. Monson
Cover Art Director: Jeff A. Storm
Cover Art Designer: Blukazoo Design
Print Production Artist: Susan Tripp
Production Manager: Dodie Tipton

ISBN 0-7644-2528-5
10 9 8 7   12 11 10 09 08 07
Printed in the United States of America.

Table of Contents

Congratulations on your new commitment to

Jesus Christ! By choosing to follow Jesus, you've made the biggest decision ever in your life. And you've entered the most exciting adventure in the universe!

Your next thirty days on this lifetime journey are critical. That's why we've written this book for you. Each day for thirty days, it gives you a helpful section on a different aspect of a Jesus-follower's life.

As you go through *A Fresh Start,* try to cover one section every single day—not just when you get around to it. Time alone with God first thing in the morning is usually best. It can set your mind right for the whole day. Get in the habit of thinking, *Bible before breakfast.* If you can't make that happen, spend time with God at the end of the day before you go to bed.

Each day's reading begins with gutsy questions and introduces issues that most new Christians face but may be afraid to ask. Gaining an understanding of what you'll face as a follower of Jesus and finding answers to your questions will help keep you from getting derailed or discouraged.

A section at the end of each day's reading will help you make the reading personal. You'll answer a question or two in writing; then you'll write your own prayer to God, including some things you've learned that day. Don't skip over this stuff. This is where it gets really practical. And often it's where God will speak to you most powerfully.

As you begin, it's important to have a Bible that's easy for you to under-stand. Here are some of the best ones, which you'll see quoted in this book. Each one is a different Bible translation. Although each sounds a little different from the others, they all teach the same things.

Contemporary English Version (CEV)
The Living Bible (LB)
New International Revised Version (NIrV)
New International Version (NIV)
New Living Translation (NLT)

Reading a portion of this book daily will get you in the habit of spending time with God every day. When you're finished you'll be well on your way to growing into all that God has created you to be.

So…let's get started!
Scott

Will It Always Feel This Way?

Dear God...

I feel great! I feel such peace and joy in my life right now. You just seem so close to me. So many people had told me how much you love me. And that you had a plan for my life. How come I could never see it before? I just couldn't understand then what I can suddenly see and accept now. I don't ever want to lose this feeling. I don't ever again want to doubt that you're for real.

Will it always feel this way?

The Bible Says...

"What happiness for those whose guilt has been forgiven! What joys when sins are covered over! What relief for those who have confessed their sins and God has cleared their record" (Psalm 32:1-2, LB).

So What Does It Mean?

Do you believe that God has forgiven you for every sin you've ever committed? Do you believe he has taken away your burden of guilt and shame? He has! Knowing and believing this brings great happiness and joy. And having the Holy Spirit living inside of us gives joy we never had before.

So, will these good feelings never end? Well...uh...no. Feelings change. A lot. Sometimes every day. Sometimes every hour. Even for Christians.

Times come when we don't feel like praying. When we don't want to go to Bible study, or get together with other Christians. That's why we don't want to put our trust in our feelings. If we do, our faith will be just as up and down as our feelings are.

Instead we must lean on the truths of the Bible. The Bible is God's personal letter to us. In it we learn who we are as his children. We learn who God is as our Father. And we can know about all the promises that are ours for both this life and the next. Trusting in these truths helps bring peace and joy no matter what we're feeling. No matter what's happening around us!

Making It Personal

Now, let's make it a bit more personal. List some things that give you peace and joy.

Pray

Dear God,

Thank you for all your amazing gifts to me. Teach me how to use these gifts in my life every day.

Write the promises that are yours today as God's child, and thank God for them.

Why Do I Feel More Guilty Now?

Dear God...

I'm so frustrated! I got mad and swore at my mom today. There's nothing really unusual about that—except that today I feel really bad about it.

That's been happening to me a lot lately. It seems like I feel guilty all the time when I'm just doing the same things I've always done. I hate that!

I feel like my actions haven't changed much since I made this new commitment. But at least before I didn't feel so bad when I did bad things!

The Bible Says...

"Those who become Christians become new persons. They are not the same anymore, for the old life is gone. A new life has begun!" (2 Corinthians 5:17b, NLT).

So What Does It Mean?

The Bible says you become a brand new person when you become a Christian. You might look the same on the outside. You might even have the same habits, concerns, and problems. But at the same time, everything is different. It's all new. You've never been this way before.

When you put your trust in Jesus, you asked him to take over the controls of your life. He takes that very seriously! So seriously, in fact, that he sent the Holy Spirit into your life. He's the one who's making you feel guilty when you do wrong. Feeling guilty is, in itself, a sure sign that God *really* is working in your life!

Now that you're a new person in Christ, it's natural for you to do what's right and not what's wrong. That doesn't mean you'll never be tempted to do wrong things. But God also promises us his power. His power helps us do the things we know we're supposed to do. How? We just need to turn to him and trust him. He'll help us not to do things that are wrong.

Just keep trusting him. Listen to the thoughts he puts in your heart. And above all, don't give up! The journey ahead of you is far better than you could ever imagine!

Making It Personal

List some of your old ways of thinking, talking, or acting that frustrate you.

What signs do you see that God has truly come into your life and made you a new person?

Pray

Dear God,

Thank you because you do live inside of me. Thanks for letting me know when I sin. I ask you to forgive me for those sins.

List specific sins and negative patterns that may have been a part of your life for a while. Ask God to help you overcome them.

Why Does My Past Still Torment Me?

Dear God...

Something's bothering me. I've noticed that Christians throw around the word forgiveness *a lot. But I'm still pretty confused about what it means.*

For one thing, if I've been truly forgiven, why do I still feel guilty about things I've done? I mean, it seems like every time I start to feel close to you at church or in prayer out come the feelings of guilt and shame again.

Soon I'm thinking about all the bad stuff I've done in the past, and then I feel like I need to ask for forgiveness all over again. Am I forgiven or not? And if so, why don't I feel free of the guilt? Help!

The Bible Says...

"So if the Son sets you free, you will be free indeed" (John 8:36, NIV).

So What Does It Mean?

The Bible tells us that all of our sins are forgiven the moment we turn our lives over to Jesus Christ—and that we are free from them. All of them! That's what Jesus' dying on the cross was all about.

I like the way 2 Corinthians 5:21 says it: "God took the sinless Christ and poured into him our sins. Then, in exchange, he poured God's goodness into us!" (LB). Wow, what an exchange that was! God took our sin upon himself, and in exchange, he gave us all of Jesus' goodness and holiness!

So why don't we always *feel* holy and free and forgiven—especially when it comes to some of those dark things from our past? First of all, the Bible says that Satan is the master accuser. He likes to bring up dirty laundry from our past. He knows it can discourage us and keep us feeling defeated. I've found three helpful steps:

1. Decide to stand upon what the Bible says: "So there is now no condemnation awaiting those who belong to Christ Jesus" (Romans 8:1, LB). Trust God's Word.

2. When a bad memory comes back to your mind, don't ask God to forgive you again. Instead say, "God, *thank you* for forgiving me for that. I know I don't deserve forgiveness, but because of what your Word says, I know that you have forgiven me. And you have even forgotten that terrible thing. Thank you!"

3. Talk with another Christian you trust about what's bothering you. I remember really struggling with a sin from my past. I felt like I was a slave to my shame.

One day I decided to talk about it with a close Christian friend. I was really nervous. But after I told my friend, he said, "Scott, in the name of Jesus, I tell you *you're forgiven.*"

I felt as if a ton of bricks just fell off my shoulders. And I never again struggled with feeling guilty about that past sin. I found the freedom promised in James 5:16, which says, "Confess your sins to each other and pray for each other so that you may be healed" (NIV).

Making It Personal

What things from your past still bother you from time to time?

Do you believe God has forgiven you for those things? Is there another step you need to take? Do you need to make it right with someone you've hurt or who has hurt you? If so, what do you need to do?

Pray

Dear God,

Thank you so much for your forgiveness. I must admit that sometimes it just seems too good to be true. I guess that's one of the things that makes you so great.

Write several specific things God has forgiven you for, and thank God for his forgiveness. Include those things you wrote down earlier. Ask him for the power to forgive yourself, if you haven't been able to do that.

What Is God Like?

Dear God...

Now that I'm a Christian, I hear a lot about what you're like. What I hear most is that you're a heavenly Father. That's kind of hard for me to relate to. You see, my father isn't exactly the kind of person I hope you're like. In fact, whenever I think about you as a heavenly Father, I get a lot of bad feelings. It makes me feel more distant, rather than closer to you.

Is there a better way of thinking about what you're like?

The Bible Says...

"A father to the fatherless, a defender of widows, is God in his holy dwelling" (Psalm 68:5, NIV).

"Now that we are his children, God has sent the Spirit of his Son into our hearts. And his Spirit tells us that God is our Father" (Galatians 4:6, CEV).

So What Does It Mean?

There is no way we can describe God fully. Anything we try falls short. He is so far above and beyond what our earthly minds can handle.

Yet our words and earthly ideas are all we have to try to explain him. That's why the Bible uses *king, lord, comforter, counselor, shepherd, mother, friend—* even *husband*. But the most common image the Bible uses to describe God *is* that of a father.

Of course, every earthly father, no matter how good he may be, falls far short when compared to our heavenly Father. Humans are sinful and limited. God is not. Let's think about what a father is *supposed* to be to us. Then we can get some idea of what God is like. Think about what the perfect father would be like. Your heart will then begin to lead you into a deeper understanding of who God is.

God is all powerful, and he's able to protect and defend us. God knows everything and sees what we cannot, so he's able to guide us perfectly.

God is completely fair and just. At the same time, he is full of love, mercy, and kindness toward us, his children. God is totally committed to us. He would never abandon us or do anything to hurt us. God is all-loving and loves most to "hold us in his arms."

Making It Personal

Think about what you already know about God. Think about what the ideal father would be to you. Then complete this sentence.

As my heavenly Father, you are...

Pray

Try to imagine that you are a child sitting on God's lap right now. Think about what you would say to your heavenly Father and write it here.

What Does God
Think About Me?

Dear God...

Is it true that you know everything about me? about my past? about what I'm involved in now and what I'm thinking about? even my future? If so, then I'm thinking you must be pretty disappointed in what you know and see.

Most people who like me wouldn't if they knew everything about me. Just thinking about what "everything" includes makes me despise myself.

The Bible Says...

"How precious it is, Lord, to realize that you are thinking about me constantly! I can't even count how many times a day your thoughts turn towards me. And when I waken in the morning, you are still thinking of me!" (Psalm 139:17-18, LB).

"The Lord your God is with you, he is mighty to save. He will take great delight in you, he will quiet you with his love, he will rejoice over you with singing" (Zephaniah 3:17, NIV).

So What Does It Mean?

What if Jesus were to walk into your room right now? (Of course, that won't happen. The Bible says that when Jesus comes again everyone will see him at once. It will be a sign of the end times. And really, Jesus is with you all the time through the Holy Spirit, who is living in you. But just imagine it, anyway.) What do you think he would say to you?

Do you think he'd be disappointed? Would he be upset that you aren't growing more spiritually? Do you think he'd be angry about all the sin you're still wrapped up in?

Do you think he'd lecture you? Would he talk about why things aren't going better for you? Or about your need to trust him more? Do you think he'd call you a hypocrite? After all, you say you're a Christian, but your words and actions often don't show it.

Well, do you know what? Jesus could say those things to every Christian alive! But according to the Bible, he would be much more likely to put his arms around you and say, "You know, I love you so much. Last night while you were sleeping, I must have thought about you a million times. I just couldn't get my mind off of you. I know your struggles, and I hurt with you. I just want you to know that I'm here. I want you to know that everything is going to be all right."

Do you have a place in your mind for that kind of God? A God who knows you so completely and yet loves you that much? A God who rejoices over you with singing, as the verse from Zephaniah says? Who not only loves you, but also *likes* you? He does. He really does!

How can that be when he knows all my sin and failures? you might ask. But that's the whole point of why Jesus died on the cross: He died to pay for our sins and failures. Because of the Cross, you are completely clean and accepted in God's sight. And rather than being a slave to your old ways, you have the power he has given you to do what's right. Does that mean you'll never mess up again? No. We all mess up, over and over and over. But know and believe this: God is still for you! He's not mad at you or fed up with you. Confess every sin. Ask his forgiveness. Accept it. Forgive yourself. Then get on with the great life he wants for you.

Making It Personal

How do you think God sees you right now?

Why?

Pray

Dear Lord,

Your never-failing love for me is almost too much for me to accept! You don't give me what I deserve when I mess up. Instead of punishing me, you show me love and you accept me.

Write a prayer thanking God for how he sees you, using such words as *forgiven, accepted,* and *the apple of my eye.* Ask God to help you see yourself more as he sees you. Ask him for new power to live so that your actions are more in line with how he sees you.

Is There Really a Devil?

Dear God...

I feel puzzled. I definitely believe in you. But I'm not so sure what to make of all this talk about a devil or Satan. Is he for real? And if so, what's he like?

The Bible Says...

"Be careful—watch out for attacks from Satan, your great enemy. He prowls around like a hungry, roaring lion, looking for some victim to tear apart" (1 Peter 5:8, LB).

"Resist the devil, and he will flee from you" (James 4:7b, NIV).

So What Does It Mean?

Interestingly, Satan is most effective when he keeps Christians from believing in him. As long as we don't recognize him or his ways, we won't resist him, as James 4:7 calls us to do.

So who is this devil anyway? What do you need to know about him? The Bible has a lot to say about Satan:

1. *He rebelled against God.* Way back, before the creation of the world, Satan was an angel in heaven. But he rebelled against God and was thrown out of heaven. A third of the angels (those who were rebelling with Satan) were thrown out with him (Revelation 12:7-9). We call Satan's angels demons.

2. *His purpose is evil.* The Bible makes clear what Satan's purpose is: to kill, steal, and destroy (John 10:10). He is the father of all lies (John 8:44) and is determined to destroy us (1 Peter 5:8).

3. *We are no match for Satan on our own.* Satan lives in the spirit world. He has powers we cannot match with our own strength. We can be sure that he knows our weaknesses and will attack us (Acts 19:13-16). Don't mess around in Satan's camp. Don't take part in séances, play with Ouija boards and tarot cards, or fool with psychics, witchcraft, or Wicca. If you've done these things in your past, meet with a pastor or Christian leader who has helped other people who've been involved in Satanic activities.

4. *He has limitations.* Satan and his demons are not equal to God. God is stronger. When we call upon God's power, demonic forces must obey and flee (Luke 9:1, 10:17-20; James 4:7).

5. *Satan will lose.* In the end, Satan and his forces of evil will be destroyed forever (Revelation 20:10).

Making It Personal

List things from your past that might have given the devil a place in your life.

Now determine to rid yourself of each of these things. Declare that their power is broken by the power of Jesus' death and resurrection.

Pray

Dear Lord,

Thank you because you alone are God. Thank you because nothing can separate me from your love and the purposes you have for me.

Write about those areas of your life where the devil has gained a hold, and give each one to God. Call on God's power to defeat the devil in each area. Ask for his power to keep you from falling today.

What's the Right Way to Pray?

Dear God...

I feel discouraged. It seems that whenever I try to pray something distracts me. Sometimes I fall asleep. Other times my mind just wanders to a hundred other things. Maybe it's because I'm talking to someone I can't see. Maybe it's because I'm not hearing right back. But I know that I need to pray. What can help me focus better?

The Bible Says...

"The prayer of a godly person is powerful. It makes things happen" (James 5:16b, NIrV).

So What Does It Mean?

Prayer is the most powerful force in the world. That's why Satan attacks it so much. The devil knows that when we pray things happen. So it shouldn't surprise us that our minds wander more than ever when we begin to pray. And like anything that's worthwhile, developing an effective prayer life takes discipline.

There's no one right way to pray. Prayer is simply talking to God as you would to your best friend. And listening to him as a friend. But sometimes having a guide can be helpful. That's what Jesus' disciples were looking for when they asked him to teach them how to pray. His answer was to give them the Lord's Prayer. This prayer is sort of an outline to follow. It can help us keep our minds on track.

Making It Personal

Try writing your own prayer beside each line of the Lord's Prayer. That's a great way to keep on track.

For example:

1. Our Father in heaven,	Heavenly Father, you are…
2. hallowed be Your name.	I praise you for…
3. Your kingdom come. Your will be done on earth as it is in heaven.	I ask for your will to be done in…
4. Give us this day our daily bread.	I ask you to meet these needs…
5. And forgive us our debts,	I confess these sins to you…
6. as we forgive our debtors.	I forgive…for…
7. And do not lead us into temptation, but deliver us from the evil one.	Help me overcome these temptations…
8. For Yours is the kingdom and the power and the glory forever. Amen. (Matthew 6:9-13, NKJV)	I release all these matters into your hands.

Pray

In addition to praying your new prayer based on the Lord's Prayer, try saying or writing one of the eight parts and then being quiet. Think about what the words mean. Let God speak to you while you try to listen to him and write down what he says. Repeat this for another part and then another.

Does God Answer All My Prayers?

Dear God...

I'm just not sure. I know I'm supposed to have faith when I pray. But it's hard to have faith when some of my prayers are answered and some aren't. Am I doing something wrong? Am I expecting too much?

The Bible Says...

"If you remain joined to me and my words remain in you, ask for anything you wish. And it will be given to you" (John 15:7, NIrV).

So What Does It Mean?

God makes some pretty bold promises about our prayers being answered, doesn't he? But he also places some conditions on his promises. It would be terrible if just anybody could pray anything and God had to fulfill it. The verse above says that we must be walking close to God if our prayers are to be effective. We must be drawing our strength from God and praying according to what he wants for us.

The Bible lists a few other conditions as well:

- that we have a relationship with God through Jesus Christ (John 10:26-27)
- that we ask in faith (James 1:5-8)
- that we aren't asking selfishly (James 4:3)
- that we don't give up (Luke 18:7)
- that we ask according to God's will (1 John 5:14-15)

We're called to keep close to God, keep praying, and leave the results up to him. As we do, we can know this for sure: Our prayers will bring about things that could never happen in any other way!

So does that mean we will always get just what we want, when we want it? Not necessarily.

Often God's answer is yes, and he was just waiting for us to ask. At other times, like any loving parent, God says no to our requests. *He* knows what's best for us; sometimes *we* don't. We just know what we want.

And sometimes the answer is wait. It's hard to wait for God's time. We want what we want now! But God's timing is always best. He's never late. He's right on time.

The more we grow in our faith the better able we are to accept all three answers to prayer: yes, no, and wait. And the more comfort we receive from the fact that God always wants what is best for us—whatever the answer is!

Making It Personal

Make a list of some things you've prayed for since you became a Christian. How have they been answered?

What are some people or situations you believe God wants you to pray for now?

Pray

Dear God,

Thank you so much for the privilege of prayer. To think that I can reach you, the Creator of the universe, "24/7" blows my mind!

Write a prayer committing to God each of the people and situations you listed.

How Does God
Speak to Me?

Dear God...

I don't get it. I hear lots of Christians talk about how God spoke to them and told them this or that. Do you speak to them out loud? What are they talking about?

The Bible Says...

"You said to me, 'I will point out the road that you should follow. I will be your teacher and watch over you' " (Psalm 32:8, CEV).

So What Does It Mean?

God speaks in many ways. But he seldom speaks in a voice we can hear with our ears the way we hear one another. Instead, God usually speaks to us through:

1. the Bible (Psalm 119:105),
2. prayer (Philippians 4: 6,7),
3. other people (Proverbs 15:22),
4. things that happen (Proverbs 19:21), and
5. speaking directly to our hearts or minds (John 10:27).

So why would God choose to communicate like this? Why not through more direct and obvious means? God says in Jeremiah 29:13, "You will seek me and find me when you seek me with all your heart" (NIV). Hearing God through his Word, in prayer, through others, through events, and in our hearts requires that we really spend time seeking *him,* not just the answers we're looking for. Maybe that's the biggest reason God speaks to us the way he does: We need God far more than we need answers!

Making It Personal

In what ways have you heard God speak and direct you?

In what area do you need God to speak to you now?

Pray

Lord,

I thank you because you do speak to me. Because you want to talk to me even more than I want to hear from you.

Write a prayer asking God to speak clearly to you in the areas where you most need his guidance today. Then take time to listen for his answers, and write down what you hear.

How Do I Know the Bible Is Really True?

Dear God...

I know that the Bible is a really important book. But it seems like some Christians almost worship it. There are a lot of good books, but people don't center their entire lives on other books the way some people center their lives on the Bible. Even if it was inspired by you, that was a long time ago! How does anyone know for sure it's all still true?

The Bible Says...

"The whole Bible was given to us by inspiration from God and is useful to teach us what is true and to make us realize what is wrong in our lives; it straightens us out and helps us do what is right" (2 Timothy 3:16, LB).

So What Does It Mean?

You're right. Christians do put a lot of stock in the Bible. That's because God tells us that it's a book like no other. It contains sixty-six separate books and letters written over a period of sixteen hundred years. Some forty different people wrote it as God spoke to them.

The books are divided into the Old Testament, or Covenant, (before Jesus' life on earth) and the New Testament (during and after Jesus' life on earth).

The books of the Bible were written in different languages, places, circumstances, and periods of time. All of the Bible's books and letters fit together to give us a clearer picture of who God is and who we are as his children.

Some people have wondered how the Bible could have been copied over so many hundreds of years without being filled with errors (no copy machines or faxes back then!). Amazingly, handwritten scrolls of several books of the Bible were found in the 1940s in a cave in the Middle East. They dated back more than two thousand years.

Scholars began to translate these Dead Sea Scrolls, as they came to be called. People were eager to see if there were differences between what we have today and what was written two thousand years ago.

What were the findings? Each of the Dead Sea Scrolls that has been translated to date is essentially the same as what we read today. Many scholars who don't believe the Bible is the Word of God admit that preserving such accuracy borders on the miraculous!

Truly God has had his hand on his Word through the centuries. And that Word applies to the everyday situations of your life and mine just as much as it did to our brothers and sisters who lived by it thousands of years ago. If you haven't read it for a while (or ever), pick it up. Start by reading the book of John. And as you read it, think of the Bible as a letter written by God to you personally. That will help to make it come alive all the more.

Making It Personal

What are some things God has taught you through his Word?

What can you do to help make sure you read the Bible every day?

Pray

Dear Lord,

Thank you for your Word, the Bible. You have promised that you will teach me through your Holy Spirit as I read it.

Write a prayer committing to a realistic plan for reading some of the Bible every day. Ask God for the power to make Bible reading a daily habit.

Do I Have to
Go to Church?

Dear God...

I know I should probably go to church, but it just seems boring. Church doesn't speak to me and my needs. I don't feel like I have anything in common with the people at the church I go to, but I don't know where else to go.

The Bible Says...

"Let us not neglect our church meetings, as some people do, but encourage and warn each other, especially now that the day of his coming back again is drawing near" (Hebrews 10:25, LB).

"They spent their time learning from the apostles, and they were like family to each other. They also broke bread and prayed together" (Acts 2:42, CEV).

So What Does It Mean?

God never intended for us to make it in the Christian life alone. We need one another. A saying I've heard goes like this: "If you want to see what your life will be like in the future, look at your friends today." The Bible says it even more bluntly: "Bad company corrupts good character" (1 Corinthians 15:33, NIV).

One of the best ways to grow strong in your faith is to hang around with others who are growing strong in their faith. A good youth group can help you grow strong in your faith. So can a church that teaches about how to grow closer to Jesus. An older spiritual mentor can be helpful too. People who don't tap into what others can offer don't make it. Or at least they don't grow much spiritually.

What if you don't feel you can grow in the church you're attending? Then ask God to lead you to another church where you can grow. It's important. In fact, I have never met a mature, strong Christian who was not connected to a good local church.

To be honest, though, there are still lots of Sundays I don't feel like going to church. There are plenty of evenings I don't want to meet with my small-group Bible study. And I've been a Christian for more than thirty years! But I've learned that, when I go in spite of my feelings, God usually gives me just what I needed for that time in my life. And he always surprises me with a blessing.

Making It Personal

Which church, youth group, and/or adult spiritual mentor is God leading you toward?

What's the next step God may want you to take in each of these areas?

Pray

Dear God,

Thank you for placing us in "spiritual families" that care for us and help us grow. Show me where you want me to receive more from other Christians. Show me where you want me to be giving more to build up your family.

Write a prayer of commitment that includes the steps you believe God is asking you to take to grow more spiritually.

How Do I Develop the Friendships I Need in My Life?

Dear God...

I feel lonely. Following you is harder than I thought it was going to be. A lot of my friends don't seem to understand or care that I'm a Christian and that I want to live your way. And sometimes I feel myself being pulled into doing things I shouldn't do. I know I need much more from my friendships now. But how do I develop friendships that will really help me grow closer to you?

The Bible Says...

"As iron sharpens iron, so one person sharpens another" (Proverbs 27:17, NIrV).

"Therefore confess your sins to each other and pray for each other so that you may be healed" (James 5:16a, NIV).

So What Does It Mean?

Being part of a small group of trusted Christian friends who are committed to God and to one another is the best recipe I know for personal spiritual growth.

For nine years, my wife and I ran a discipleship home for boys coming out of juvenile jails. John was one of the first boys who lived with us. Shortly after he moved in, he said, "I don't think God is going to move any of us to a deeper level spiritually until we're all together." He was right on target. The others in our home agreed. Together we developed the Covenant of Commitment, which each of us signed. The covenant is on the next page.

Not every group of guys in our home was ready for this covenant or even wanted it. But for those who did, the covenant produced more spiritual growth than any other thing we did.

Making It Personal

Do you feel you're ready? Do you want this type of commitment and accountability with a small group of Christian friends? Why or why not?

Covenant of Commitment

1. I'm asking you to love me enough to tell me the truth about myself as you see it. *"Wounds from a friend can be trusted, but an enemy multiplies kisses" (Proverbs 27:6, NIV).*

2. I love you enough to commit to confronting you about things I'm concerned about in your life. *"Better is open rebuke than hidden love" (Proverbs 27:5, NIV).*

Weekly Questions to Ask One Another

1. How have you been doing recently in the areas of temptation with drugs, alcohol, sex, or foul language?

2. How has your attitude been this week toward family, work, friends, and yourself?

3. Is there somebody you need to forgive or ask forgiveness from?

4. How has your time with God been this week? What has been your experience with prayer, reading your Bible, and having time alone?

5. What kinds of negative things have you allowed into your mind this week? (Think about the impact of music, movies, TV, magazines, and peers.)

6. Is there any area in which you think God is asking you to take another step?

If you're ready for this kind of group, who might be willing to be in it with you? (For open sharing in these groups, it's important that all members be of the same sex.)

Pray

Dear God,

Please give me the "iron sharpening iron" kind of friendships. Lead me to the right people so that I can grow spiritually. I want to be all that you have in mind for me to become.

Write a prayer to God and include those key people he has put in your heart to help you grow. Pray for each of them and for God's help in bringing you together.

How Do I Know What God Wants Me to Do?

Dear God...

*I keep hearing people say that you have this wonderful plan for my life. I just have one question: **What** is it? I guess what I mean is, How do I find out what your plan is for my life? And just how detailed is it? Does it include things like who I'm supposed to marry? What job I'm supposed to have? What school I should attend?*

Or is it more general, like just living a good life? Is this plan something I can easily miss? Or is it more like fate—whatever's supposed to happen will just happen if I believe in you?

The Bible Says...

" 'For I know the plans I have for you,' declares the Lord, 'plans to prosper you and not to harm you, plans to give you hope and a future' " (Jeremiah 29:11, NIV).

So What Does It Mean?

How can I know what God's will is for my life? This is perhaps the number one question Christians ask. And it's a great question. Why? Because God wants to show his will to us even more than we want to know it. So, how does it happen?

First: God's will for us begins with what is general and true for all Christians. For example, 1 Thessalonians 5:16-18 says, "Be joyful always; pray continually; give thanks in all circumstances, for this is God's will for you in Christ Jesus" (NIV). This and many other Scriptures explain God's will for all of his children. God will never tell you something or lead you in a way that's different from what's in his Word. So start by getting to know God's will for you through the Bible.

Second: Ask God for his detailed leading and direction. In James 1:5 he promises that, if we lack wisdom, we should ask him and he will give it to us generously if we ask and believe.

Third: Get to know yourself. God has made you unique. He has never created another person just like you in all of history. And he made you for a purpose that no one else can accomplish! The Bible says that every one of us has spiritual gifts. They're listed in Romans 12:6-8; 1 Corinthians 12:8-10, 28; and Ephesians 4:11-13. If you don't know what gifts God has given you, ask your pastor or youth leader to help you find out.

Fourth: Ask other Christians who know you well to give you honest feedback about where they see your gifts, passions, and abilities. People who know you can often see things you can't as they observe you over time.

Fifth: Step out and try different things. The best way to discover the unique calling God has for your life is to take part in different ministry opportunities whenever you can. Here are some ideas to think about. Go on mission trips. Help teach a children's Sunday school class. Help feed the homeless or visit shut-ins. Help in the media department at church. As you serve God in different ways, you'll learn a great deal. You'll begin to sense how God works through you best. You'll learn where you feel happiest and most fulfilled. You'll discover gifts you never knew you had.

God says that we should be faithful in little things. Then he will lead us to and entrust us with bigger things—things like which college we should attend, what career path we should take, and who our future husband or wife should be.

Making It Personal

List some of the characteristics God has put together in this unique human being called YOU.

• my strengths:

• my natural abilities:

• types of people I'm good with:

• what I'm really passionate about:

• some of my most fulfilling experiences:

• what makes me happy:

Pray

Lord,

You made me who I am. I'm yours. You've given me gifts, abilities, and a calling in life that make me unique.

Ask God to show you even more of his will for your life. Write down specific areas where you need his guidance right now.

Why Do I Keep
Messing Up?

Dear God...

I feel defeated. You must be getting pretty tired of me. I can see how you might forgive me once, twice, even three times. But I keep falling into the same old sin over and over. At what point have you had enough? When do you refuse to keep forgiving me?

The Bible Says...

"He has removed our sins as far away from us as the east is from the west" (Psalm 103:12, LB).

"But I wipe away your sins because of who I am. And so, I will forget the wrongs you have done" (Isaiah 43:25, CEV).

So What Does It Mean?

One of the main differences between how we forgive and how God forgives is this: We can't always forget. He can.

When I was a teenager, I struggled with a certain sin over and over again. The pattern was painfully familiar. I would mess up. Then I would feel really guilty. Out of my guilt, I would cry out to God for forgiveness. I would promise to him and myself that I would never do it again.

That process would bring great relief, peace, and victory. Sometimes it would last for as long as a few days or even a few weeks or months. But eventually I seemed to fall back into the same old sin again.

I repeated this process more times than I care to remember. I finally gave up on myself and my ability to break this sinful pattern. "God doesn't want to hear from me again," I reasoned. "And I'm not going to humiliate myself by coming back and confessing the same old thing one more time."

As a result I began to distance myself from God. The results were painful. I felt more lonely, isolated, and defeated than ever.

Finally in desperation I came back to God. "Lord, I'm so sorry. Again and again I have fallen into this sin. I'm so embarrassed I can hardly talk to you, for I've done it again..." Just then I felt as if God was saying to my heart, "You've done what? I don't remember that sin." Later I discovered the amazing truth the Scriptures tell us about God's forgiveness. God not only forgives, he forgets!

I also found that knowing how God saw me gave me the courage I needed to deal head-on with my sin patterns rather than deny them. I learned to enlist others in healthy accountability and to trust in God's power to free me from those sins that had enslaved me for so long.

Making It Personal

What sins cause you to feel defeated?

Does it help to know that God has completely forgiven and forgotten your past offenses? Explain.

Pray

Oh Lord,

I can hardly fathom that all of my sins have been forgiven—and forgotten because of your blood on the cross. You know I don't want to be bound by my sins any longer. So I bring myself to you again today. Thank you for giving me a completely clean life once again.

Write a prayer asking God for his power over the temptations and issues you know will likely come up for you today. Be specific.

If God Accepts Me Anyway, Why Not Keep on Sinning?

Dear God...

I hear a lot of talk about being forgiven and accepted by you no matter what I do. But if that's the case, why stress out so much about trying to do good? If you will always forgive me, what does it hurt if I sin?

The Bible Says...

"So since God's grace has set us free from the law, does this mean we can go on sinning? Of course not! Don't you realize that whatever you choose to obey becomes your master? You can choose sin, which leads to death, or you can choose to obey God and receive his approval" (Romans 6:15-16a, NLT).

"Christ has set us free. He wants us to enjoy freedom. So stand firm. Don't let the chains of slavery hold you again" (Galatians 5:1, NIrV).

"You must display a new nature because you are a new person, created in God's likeness—righteous, holy, and true" (Ephesians 4:24, NLT).

So What Does It Mean?

It's really important for every Christian to understand that as God's children we're completely forgiven, accepted, and made right with God. That's what happened on the cross when "Christ didn't have any sin. But God made him become sin for us. So we can be made right with God because of what Christ has done for us" (2 Corinthians 5:21 NIrV).

Jesus' death on the cross for our sins makes it possible for us to have a close personal relationship with God while we're here on earth. And it's why we can spend eternity in heaven with him when we die. But the Apostle Paul also said, "Only let us live up to what we have already attained" (Philippians 3:16, NIV). In other words, because we have been made right with God and acceptable, we can now also act like it.

When the Bible speaks about being a slave, it's usually talking about being bound by sin. But when it speaks about freedom, it's talking about having the power to do what is right (John 8:36). Before coming to Christ, we were all slaves to sin. But now we have both the desire and the supernatural power to turn away from sin. Now we can live lives for good and not evil. Now we can be truly free.

Here's another way to say it. Before we came to Christ, it was natural for us to

DAY 15

do wrong. Now it is more natural to do right. So why would we ever go back to being bound by those harmful, sinful patterns just because we can be forgiven for them? There's no good reason. The temptation to go back will always be there, but God's power to keep us from it is stronger.

Making It Personal

How have your wants changed since you invited Jesus to take over your life?

God accepts you and loves you completely—no matter what. How does knowing this empower you to do the right things?

Pray

Oh Lord,

Thank you for the freedom you have given me. Thanks for the new desires you've put in my heart. Make those desires even stronger.

Write a prayer, listing the new desires God has put into your life. Ask him for the faith and strength to follow those desires today.

What's the
Holy Spirit?

Dear God...

I'm confused. Christians talk a lot about the Holy Spirit. Is that a force or a part of you or what? Or is it just another name for you?

The Bible Says...

"But when the Father sends the Comforter instead of me [Jesus]—and by the Comforter I mean the Holy Spirit—he will teach you much, as well as remind you of everything I myself have told you" (John 14:26, LB).

So What Does It Mean?

The Holy Spirit is not a force. He is a person. God is made up of three persons in one being: The Father, Jesus the Son, and the Holy Spirit. Together they're called the Trinity, which means "three in one." I admit, it does sound pretty confusing! All three have always existed, but each has a different role. Throughout the Old Testament, we read mostly about God the Father. Jesus' words in the New Testament tell us more about God the Father.

We read about Jesus in the New Testament, which tells about his being born as a baby on earth and then as an adult dying on the cross for our sins.

We read about the Holy Spirit mostly in the New Testament too. Though the Holy Spirit has always existed and acted in our world, he was sent to earth in a special way after Jesus went back to heaven. The Holy Spirit is the one who draws us to God. He lives inside all who receive Jesus as Lord of their lives. He teaches us, guides us, and gives us strength. He shows us when we sin and get off course.

He helps us to know and feel God's presence. The Bible calls the Holy Spirit a counselor and a helper. The Holy Spirit's presence in us is important to all we do. It's just as important to get to know him as it is to know Jesus and the Father.

Making It Personal

How have you felt the Holy Spirit work in your life?

Pray

Dear Holy Spirit,

I want to get to know you a lot better. Help me to know when you're speaking to me.

Write a prayer to the Holy Spirit asking him to guide, teach, and help you to do God's will today. Be specific about the areas in which you need him most.

How Can God Understand What I'm Going Through?

Dear God...

Sometimes you seem so far away. I know you love me a lot. It's just that I don't always feel like you can relate to what I'm going through right here and now.

The Bible Says...

"And it was necessary for Jesus to be like us…For since he himself has now been through suffering and temptation, he knows what it is like when we suffer and are tempted, and he is wonderfully able to help us" (Hebrews 2:17-18, LB).

"[Jesus] understands our weaknesses, since he had the same temptations we do, though he never once gave way to them and sinned" (Hebrews 4:15, LB).

So What Does It Mean?

Back in the 1990s Bette Midler recorded a song by Julie Gold titled "From a Distance," which includes the words, "God is watching us from a distance." It's a cool song. But it falls far short in describing God. Jesus' coming to earth was more than just his dying on the cross to pay for our sins. It was even more than his being brought back to life. God could have done that in heaven in just a second. It could have been done without Jesus having to suffer all that he did while he lived on earth for thirty-three years.

According to what the Bible says, Jesus had to suffer in every way that we suffer and be tempted in every way that we are tempted so he could understand what we are going through and walk with us through it.

Think about that. Everything you or I go through, Jesus understands. He has also faced the kinds of temptations you and I face. Consider some of what he faced on earth. He was born to an unmarried teenage mother. He was born into the most hated race in the world at that time. He died one of the most cruel and horrible types of death in the history of mankind. His friends abandoned him in his most needy moment, as did his Father. God, the Father, had to look away while the sins of mankind were put upon Jesus on the cross.

What kind of person do you look for when you're going through something really hard? Someone who is known for giving advice on every topic? Or someone who has gone through the same thing you're going through—and gotten through it?

Making It Personal

What are you going through right now that you need Jesus to understand?

How did he handle situations like yours?

How do you think he can help you with what you're going through?

Pray

Lord,

It's amazing that you, God, would lower yourself to become a person. It's amazing that you would suffer and be tempted so you could understand me and help me. Thanks, God.

Turn to God first, instead of last, when you need help. And start now by writing your prayer about what you need to trust him for today.

Is the Christian Life Mainly About Saying No to Everything That's Fun?

Dear God...

I feel so discouraged. Because I'm a Christian there's just so much I need to say no to. Sometimes I think that if I'd just quit doing everything fun, I'd finally be a good Christian!

The Bible Says...

"The thief comes only to steal and kill and destroy. I have come so they can have life. I want them to have it in the fullest possible way" (John 10:10, NIrV).

So What Does It Mean?

One of the devil's biggest lies is that the Christian life is mostly about saying no to everything that's fun. And making us believe we have to replace fun with what's boring or hard. Nothing could be further from the truth. God created all of us with the same desires: for fun, for purpose, for intimacy, for excitement, for acceptance, to feel good—and most of all to honor him. He has also made a way for our desires to be met: through his people and his calling on our lives and through our relationship with him.

We get into trouble when we settle for the counterfeit solutions the devil tempts us with. As the verse above says, "He comes to steal and kill and destroy." But of course, he never packages his temptations that way, or they wouldn't tempt us. Drugs, alcohol, sinful sexual activity, and other harmful behaviors are tempting. They promise to meet our deepest desires. But in the end they don't. Instead, they leave us worse off than we were.

The solution is not in saying no to your desires. It's in making your desires bigger! In other words, don't lower your expectations—increase them! God wants you to have more of what will satisfy you, not less. He says, "Why spend money on what is not bread and your labor on what does not satisfy? Listen, listen to me, and eat what is good, and your soul will delight in the richest of fare" (Isaiah 55:2, NIV).

So the Christian life is mainly about saying *yes* to the best things. And this is the amazing part. When we do that, the noes have a way of taking care of themselves, because our needs and desires are met with the real thing.

The Bible says, "But seek first his kingdom and his righteousness, and all these things will be given to you as well" (Matthew 6:33, NIV). As with many things in life, the key is putting things in the right order. In other words, when we focus on God's kingdom first, we'll get everything else we need as well.

Making It Personal

What counterfeit things have you settled for to meet your deepest desires?

In what ways do you think God wants to meet your desires?

Pray

Dear God,

Show me the big "yeses" you have for me. Increase my desire for you and what you have for me.

Ask God for the courage to say no to all the counterfeits in life. Write and present to God some of the ones you're facing most right now. Write and commit to him the yeses you believe he wants you to follow instead.

Why Is It That the Harder I Try the More I Seem to Mess Up?

Dear God...

I feel like giving up. It seems the harder I try to do what's right, the more I fail. I wasn't expecting it to be this hard. I would go so far as to say it's nearly impossible to live the Christian life.

The Bible Says...

"No matter which way I turn I can't make myself do right. I want to but I can't. When I want to do good, I don't; and when I try not to do wrong, I do it anyway...Oh, what a terrible predicament I'm in! Who will free me from my slavery to this deadly lower nature? Thank God! It has been done by Jesus Christ our Lord. He has set me free" (Romans 7:18b-19, 24-25, LB).

"I have been crucified with Christ and I no longer live, but Christ lives in me. The life I live in the body, I live by faith in the Son of God, who loved me and gave himself for me" (Galatians 2:20, NIV).

So What Does It Mean?

When you realized that it's impossible to live the Christian life, you hit the nail on the head! The Christian life is not just about doing your best to please God and trying to be a good person. It's way beyond that. So far beyond, in fact, that only Christ himself can pull it off. Sometimes as we try to live the Christian life, we don't even realize we're trying to do it on our own. As Galatians 2:20 says, our part is to allow Christ to live his life through us. That's what makes the Christian life supernatural.

Jesus never asks us to do what's impossible. Instead, he wants us to turn to him and allow him to take over in our lives. And when we do, something wonderful happens. We discover his power doing things in and through us—things that we could never pull off on our own.

Here's a prayer I've repeated hundreds of times since I first heard it years ago: *I can't. You never said I could. You can. You always said you would.*

DAY 19

Making It Personal

In what areas have you been trying to live the Christian life on your own strength?

How would these areas be different if you allowed Christ to live his life through you?

Pray

Dear Lord,

I'm sorry for trying to do your job. How foolish to think I could do what only you can do.

Write a prayer asking God to show you what each area of your life would look like if you let him live his life through you. List some of those areas.

How Can I Know That Christianity's the Right Religion?

Dear God...

I'm confused. There are so many religions out there, and some of my friends think other ones are better than Christianity. How do I know which one is right? And even if Christianity is right, does that make all the other ones wrong?

The Bible Says...

"The truth about God is plain to them. God has made it plain. Ever since the world was created it has been possible to see the qualities of God that are not seen. I'm talking about his eternal power and about the fact that he is God. Those things can be seen in what he has made. So people have no excuse for what they do" (Romans 1:19-20, NIrV).

"Jesus told him, 'I am the way, the truth, and the life. No one can come to the Father except through me' " (John 14:6, NLT).

So What Does It Mean?

Why are there so many religions in the world? Romans 1:19-20 gives us some reasons why. God has created us to know that he's there, and our hearts are drawn to worship. Everyone worships someone or something. Even those who don't believe in God worship something. It may be money, possessions, a relationship, or any of a thousand other things.

So it shouldn't be surprising that so many religions exist. But are they all on equal grounds? Is one just as right as another? This is a popular idea, but the logic doesn't hold up in any other area of life. Just because I say that for me two plus two equals five doesn't make it true. The only truth is that two plus two equals four. In the same way, while many religions claim to be *the* right one, only one can truly be right.

We should respect all people regardless of their religious beliefs. But other religions can't all be true. That's why it's so important to have an authority to stand upon. We do not just base our beliefs on what any one person might think. The Bible is the final authority for Christians.

So what is the basic difference between Christianity and other religions? There are two major differences. Many religions had great leaders, but each of those leaders died. Jesus is the only leader to come back to life. This fact is not just something Christians have to believe or accept by faith. It is a historical event supported by as much evidence as nearly any other major event in ancient history.

Here's a second major difference. Almost every religion is based upon what we must *do* to get to God. Doing more good things than bad, for example, or making sacrifices to pay for all the bad we've done. Only Christianity is based on what God *did* to bring us to him. Our part is to simply trust in what he's already done. Does that mean that God is not concerned with what we do? No. He's very concerned. But good works come as the result of our faith, not the other way around.

Making It Personal

How would you answer someone who said it doesn't matter what you believe as long as you believe in something and that all roads lead to God?

Pray

Dear God,

Thank you for showing yourself to us through all of creation, through your Word, and through our consciences. Thank you for making a way for us to come to you through your Son, Jesus Christ.

Pray for someone who doesn't know God. Write down the person's name, and ask God to show himself to him or her.

How Do I Resist Temptation?

Dear God...

I've been a Christian for a while now. Yet I feel like I'm being tempted more now than ever. Where's it all coming from? How do I resist it?

The Bible Says...

"When you are tempted, you shouldn't say, 'God is tempting me.' God can't be tempted by evil. And he doesn't tempt anyone.

"But your own evil longings tempt you. They lead you on and drag you away. When they are allowed to grow, they give birth to sin. When sin has grown up, it gives birth to death" (James 1:13-15, NIrV).

"You are tempted in the same way all other human beings are. God is faithful. He will not let you be tempted any more than you can take. But when you are tempted, God will give you a way out so that you can stand up under it" (1 Corinthians 10:13, NIrV).

So What Does It Mean?

It's true that everyone is tempted. But it's also true that Christians are often tempted even more than other people. Why is that?

Think about where temptation comes from. The Bible clearly states that *God* doesn't tempt us. Temptations come from our own evil desires and from the devil himself. Why would the devil spend energy on those who aren't causing him much of a problem? If you're tempted more than you used to be, perhaps it's because you're a problem for the devil. You may be doing more good for God's kingdom. You're creating problems for the devil, so the devil is attacking you more!

The Bible lists three main types of temptations. According to 1 John 2:16, they are

- the lusts of the flesh (for example, sex, drugs, overeating, or not eating enough),
- the lusts of the eyes (jealousy or stealing, for example), and
- pride (thinking you're better than others).

Remember reading on Day 17 about how Jesus himself went through everything we go through? He faced each of these types of temptations when he was fasting and praying for forty days. In each case he called upon God for help. He drew power and strength from God's Word (see Luke 4:1-13).

Satan knows our natural areas of weakness. That's where he'll tempt us most. But God also promises a way of escape if we turn to him and don't depend on our own strength. God keeps us from many of the temptations and bad things that could come our way. But he does allow some to come through. Why? So that we learn to depend on him for help. And in the process we grow even stronger.

Making It Personal

What temptation do you struggle with most?

How do you think God can help you with this temptation?

Pray

Lord,

Thank you for not allowing any temptation to get through to me that I can't handle with your help.

Ask God to help you with what's tempting you right now (be specific) so that you can stand up under it and even come out stronger as a result.

Why Doesn't God Just Show Himself to Me?

Dear God...

I'm so full of doubts. At first I was so sure that you are real. But now I'm beginning to wonder. Maybe it's because of what my friends say. Maybe it's just that I can't see you. What other relationship is like this? I still pray, but I can't help wondering if you're really listening. Sometimes I wish you would just show yourself so I would know for a fact that you're there.

The Bible Says...

"As long as we live in these bodies we are not at home with the Lord. That is why we live by believing and not by seeing" (2 Corinthians 5:6b-7, NLT).

"Without faith it isn't possible to please God. Those who come to God must believe that he exists. And they must believe that he rewards those who look to him" (Hebrews 11:6, NIrV).

"I do believe; help me overcome my unbelief!" (Mark 9:24b, NIV).

So What Does It Mean?

Recently I saw a bumper sticker that said, "Not seeing is believing." I had to really think about that. If you see something, you feel confident that it exists. But if you don't see something, it takes more work to believe in its existence. Sure, it would be easier if we could just see God and not have to *believe* that he's with us. But would that make us stronger followers of him? The stories in the Bible seem to say no.

One of the lowest periods of Biblical history was when Moses led the children of Israel to the land God had promised them. Because they were in a desert, God led them with a cloud during the day. At night, he set a pillar of fire before them so they could see it and follow him then, too (Exodus 13:21). And because there was no food, God dropped manna (kind of like bread) and quail (tastes like chicken!) out of the sky for them to eat (Exodus 16:4, 13).

You'd expect these people to be giants in their faith, wouldn't you? After all, God's hand was so obvious in their lives. But here's the amazing thing. There may have been four or five million Israelites who saw God's miracles every day. Yet, when it came to facing enemies in the land, only two leaders (Joshua and Caleb) had enough faith to enter into the land God had promised them.

God requires faith of us. Without it, we can't please him. Seeing doesn't always increase our faith. Believing does. And, oh, how God loves to reward us as we have faith in him.

Making It Personal

What's hardest for you to believe without seeing?

In what areas do you need to trust God more?

Pray

Lord,

Thank you for your gift of faith. I wouldn't be here or reading this book if you hadn't given me faith in you.

Write a prayer asking God to increase your faith even more. Be specific about those areas where you need the added faith most today.

What's Heaven Like?

Dear God...

All this talk about heaven is confusing to me. I feel like I should be a lot more excited about it. Especially since all the pain and suffering we experience here on earth will be gone when we get there. But there's so much good about what's here too. The picture I have of heaven seems boring compared to all the cool stuff here—like being at a concert, walking on the beach, or hanging out with good friends. Maybe it's just hard for me to get excited about something I know so little about. Is it like we'll all be sitting around with angels singing songs all day? Or is there more to it?

The Bible Says...

"There are many rooms in my Father's house. I wouldn't tell you this, unless it was true. I am going there to prepare a place for each of you. After I have done this, I will come back and take you with me. Then we will be together" (John 14:2-3, CEV).

So What Does It Mean?

The Bible doesn't say a lot about what heaven is like. It's another one of those things we must accept by faith. But if God made this world in seven days and he's been working on heaven ever since, as this verse indicates, we know it's going to be incredible!

Let's think about our frustration in comprehending what heaven will be like. In some ways it would be like trying to describe "life on the outside" to a baby still in his mother's womb. We might say, "We can't wait for you to come out here. You're gonna love it! There are beautiful trees and sunshine and wonderful people who will love you."

"What's a *tree*? What's a *sunshine*? And what's a *people*?" the little one would ask. "I like it in here where it's dark and warm. I can eat 24/7 and always hear my mom's heartbeat. Is it like that out there?"

"Well, uh, no. But..."

"Well, then, I'm not interested. I'm going to stay here."

It's hard to describe something that's so "other" to someone with such limited understanding, isn't it? John the Apostle struggled with the same thing when he wrote the Bible book of Revelation. There he tried to describe in earthly terms the vision of heaven that God had given him. Imagine his problem searching for words to explain what he was seeing. What did he come up with? A place of such beauty that it would take your breath away. A place where there are no tears and where everyone is happy and full of joy all the time.

One Sunday school teacher explained it this way: "Think of the moment in your life when you felt the most pleasure. Multiply it by a thousand. That still doesn't come close to how it will be all the time in heaven!"

There will be far more to do in heaven than just sing songs all day. Part of the joy will be that we'll rule and reign over the entire universe with God (2 Timothy 2:12; Revelation 22:5)!

Making It Personal

What do you think heaven will be like?

What do you think the Bible means when it says we are citizens of heaven and not of this world?

Pray

Lord,

Thank you because, as your child, I'm going to live in heaven forever. I don't know what it will be like. But I know it will be so much greater than all the best that this earth has to offer. Help me learn to live more as a citizen of heaven, which will last forever, than as a mere citizen of this world.

Write a prayer thanking God for heaven. List the things about it that you're most thankful for.

Why Is God So Down on Sex?

Dear God...

I'm puzzled. One of the things I hear a lot is that we're not supposed to have sex until we're married. That just seems a bit old-fashioned to me. If I really love someone, why would you want me to wait for something that's as much fun and as beautiful as sex?

The Bible Says...

"Run away from sexual sin! No other sin so clearly affects the body as this one does. For sexual immorality is a sin against your own body" (1 Corinthians 6:18, NLT).

"And don't you know that if a man joins himself to a prostitute, he becomes one body with her? For the Scriptures say, 'The two are united into one' " (1 Corinthians 6:16, NLT).

So What Does It Mean?

Sometimes it's hard to imagine God talking with us about sex. It just doesn't seem like a very godly topic. But nothing could be further from the truth. God made sex. He made it for us to enjoy.

If it's so good, why would God keep it from us until we're married? Think for a moment about how many other people you would like your future husband or wife to have had sex with before you get married. Ten? Twenty? One hundred? Everyone I've ever asked says, "None." We all know deep inside that sex with one person, in a lifetime commitment, is the ultimate relationship we can have.

That's one of the big differences between us and animals. Most animals can freely mate all their lives and without guilt or diseases or broken hearts. Not us humans. Sex is much, much bigger for us. It involves all that we are. In fact, God says that when two people have sex they become one. And it's not just about our bodies. Sex involves our spirits and souls as well.

There's no greater gift anyone could ever give a future husband or wife than the gift of virginity. It's by far the most romantic gift in the world. It also shows that you have what it takes to be faithful to your husband or wife when temptations come later in marriage.

What about those who've already lost their virginity? All month long, we've been learning that with God there's always the opportunity for a clean slate and a fresh start! If you've already had sex, accept that clean slate and seek to follow Jesus in your relationship decisions. Trust God with sex just as you do every other part of your life.

Making It Personal

What do you need God to do to restore your sexual purity?

How will you deal with sexual temptation from now on?

Pray

Thank you, God, for your beautiful gift of sex. I don't want to miss any of what you have for me in this area of my life. Give me and my future spouse the power and courage to wait for all you have for us together.

Write your own prayer of confession and commitment to God for this area of your life.

Am I Supposed to Forgive
Everything and *Everyone?*

Dear God...

There's something I've got to know. The Bible talks a lot about forgiving ourselves and others. But it's just not that easy. What about when someone has really hurt you? Are you supposed to just forget that it ever happened? What if they do it again, or if they now feel they can take advantage of you?

The Bible Says...

"Forgive the things you are holding against one another. Forgive, just as the Lord forgave you" (Colossians 3:13b, NIrV).

So What Does It Mean?

God commands us to forgive others—even our enemies according to Matthew 5:44—for at least three reasons:

1. so we might be set free from the bitterness that "eats us up" when we have anger or hatred toward another,

2. to make room for God to deal with the person (Romans 12:19a says, "Do not take revenge, my friends, but leave room for God's wrath" [NIV].), and

3. to restore a relationship.

But what about when someone continues to betray your trust or even abuses you? Forgiving someone does not mean allowing him or her to continue in the same destructive activity. Forgiving someone does not release that person from the results of his or her harmful behavior. In some cases the most loving thing to do is to report abusive behavior to those who can ensure that the abuser will not cause the same harm to others.

At other times, a solution may be as simple as not allowing that person the opportunity to hurt you again. It may take a trusted friend to help you figure out what you should do.

Of course, forgiveness is not easy. We need Jesus' help to do it. But when we don't forgive, we allow another person to take over much of our minds and control us. Resentment takes more and more of that precious space in our heads as our thoughts focus on how we can get even, or how we've been hurt. Ask God to give back to you those areas of your mind that have been robbed through bitterness and resentment.

Making It Personal

Who are you struggling most to forgive and why?

How does this struggle affect you?

Pray

Dear God,

Thanks so much for forgiving me for all the terrible things I've done in my life. Help me to be as forgiving.

Write a prayer asking God to help you forgive that person you're struggling most with right now. Write down his or her name, and ask God if there's more you need to do for that person's sake or yours. Ask God to show you if there's someone you should talk to about it. If you sense there is, write down the name and commit to talking with him or her about it today.

Why Do I Still Struggle and Have Problems?

Dear God...

I know that as a Christian I should be filled with peace and joy. But right now I'm feeling a little disillusioned. I thought that when I became a Christian I wouldn't have the same problems as before. Why do you still allow me to struggle?

The Bible Says...

"Here on earth you will have many trials and sorrows. But take heart, because I have overcome the world" (John 16:33b, NLT).

"We also rejoice in our sufferings, because we know that suffering produces perseverance; perseverance, character; and character, hope. And hope does not disappoint us" (Romans 5:3b-5a, NIV).

So What Does It Mean?

If given a choice, we would all choose not to go through suffering. And becoming a Christian should remove lots of it. Many of our problems come from our own poor choices. As we grow in Christ, the choices we make should also be changing.

Yet, there are other types of suffering that still exist for the growing Christian. One type is suffering for doing what is right. Second, we sometimes suffer from things that happen because we live in a sinful, fallen world. For example, close friends or family members die. Our hopes and dreams sometimes don't come true. Poor choices made by others can still hurt us. Terrible things still happen around us and sometimes to us.

The difference for Christians is this: While we know that God doesn't cause these bad things to happen, we also know that he promises to use them in our lives for good. That is, if we allow him to.

Below is an illustration of Romans 5:3-5.

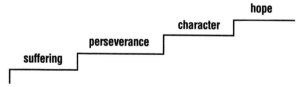

When we entrust ourselves and our trials to God, he uses them. He allows trials and suffering to produce perseverance and patience in our lives. And as we grow in perseverance, our very character is changed. We, and others, recognize that we're different than we used to be. Finally, changed character leads to hope. In the Bible, hope is not simply wishful thinking. It's being sure that God will use everything that comes our way for our good (Romans 8:28).

Making It Personal

How have you seen God work to develop perseverance, character, and hope from a struggle in your past?

What trial are you going through now that God might use to develop perseverance, character, and hope in you?

Pray

Dear Lord,
Thank you for the way I've seen you use the bad things in my life to produce so much good in me.

List the struggles you're going through right now and commit them to God. Ask him to use them to change you even more so you'll be more like Christ.

How Do I Handle My Worry and Stress?

Dear God...

I worry a lot. Is that a sin? How can you help me not worry so much?

The Bible Says...

"Look at the birds in the sky! They don't plant or harvest. They don't even store grain in barns. Yet your Father in heaven takes care of them. Aren't you worth more than birds? Can worry make you live longer?" (Matthew 6:26-27, CEV).

"Don't worry about anything; instead, pray about everything; tell God your needs and don't forget to thank him for his answers. If you do this you will experience God's peace, which is far more wonderful than the human mind can understand. His peace will keep your thoughts and your hearts quiet and at rest as you trust in Christ Jesus" (Philippians 4:6-7, LB).

So What Does It Mean?

We all worry, but no one has ever made a bad situation better by worrying. As the Bible verse says, "Can worry make you live longer?" The answer is an obvious no. Not only is worrying a waste of time, it will likely shorten your life. So don't allow it to rob your energy or your life.

Of course, all this is much easier said than done. How can we stop worrying even if we want to? According to what the Bible says, it's a matter of trust. Jesus talks about how God faithfully takes care of the birds. And he says that we are of far greater value to him than birds.

At its core, worry is a sign of not trusting God. That's the opposite of faith. And that's what makes worry a sin. Besides, it takes no more energy to pray than it does to worry. And not only does prayer change things, it changes us as well. The Bible promises us that prayer will help us have peace beyond what our human mind can understand.

Does that mean we shouldn't be concerned about anything? Does it mean that we just figure, "whatever will be, will be"? No, not at all. After talking about worry, Jesus gave us a plan that can never fail: "But put God's kingdom first. Do what he wants you to do. Then all of those things will also be given to you" (Matthew 6:33, NIrV). God will give you all you need from day to day if you live for him and make the kingdom of God your main concern. Put God first. Do what you can. Then leave the rest up to him. And when you feel worry coming on, turn it into a prayer.

Making It Personal

What things have you been worrying about a lot lately?

What do you think it means to put God's kingdom first?

What would that look like in the area that is causing you the most worry right now?

Pray

Dear Lord,

I confess that I worry more than I pray. Please forgive me and build my faith and trust in you. I want to give these areas of worry over to you right now. Thanks also for your promise to meet my needs.

List your worries and present them to God. Release them, one at a time, from your hands and place them into his.

If God Loves Everyone, Why Would He Send Some People to Hell?

Dear God...

I'm having a hard time understanding why a God who loves everyone would send people to hell if they don't believe in Jesus.

The Bible Says...

"The Lord is not slow to keep his promise. He is not slow in the way some people understand it. He is patient with you. He doesn't want anyone to be destroyed. Instead, he wants all people to turn away from their sins" (2 Peter 3:9, NIrV).

"For the wages of sin is death, but the free gift of God is eternal life through Jesus Christ our Lord" (Romans 6:23, LB).

So What Does It Mean?

It is God's desire that all people come to know him. God does not want anyone to go to hell. Hell is not some place of torture a mean God created to send people to. Rather, hell is the absence of God. And because of God's absence, hell is a place filled with all the evil, torture, and pain of this world. Except that in hell that misery is multiplied thousands of times over—and beyond.

This world has a lot of bad in it, as we know. But it also has a lot of good, as God's hand is upon it. Hell won't have any good in it. The Bible tells us that God loves every person in the world. He wants all of us to spend eternity with him in heaven.

That's why God sent Jesus to pay for our sins, which is something we could never do on our own. But God also allows each person to make choices. He does not force us to choose him or heaven. We have free will. In the end, hell is when God finally gives a person the right to tell God to leave him or her alone—for eternity. And that's what makes it hell.

That's why we need to tell people about Jesus. We need to explain the wonderful offer he gives each of us. This offer is not only to escape hell, but also to experience his abundant goodness in this life and the next.

Making It Personal

List some of the people you care about who have rejected Jesus' offer to forgive their sins and give them a new life. What do you want them to know?

Pray

Dear Lord,

I know that I deserve hell. You said that it is the penalty for sin. Thank you so much for showing Jesus to me. Thank you because he has forgiven me and made me right in your sight.

Write a prayer for your friends and family who don't yet understand what God has done for us. Ask God to give you an opportunity to share with them.

How Do I Explain This Stuff to My Friends and Family?

Dear God...

I'm concerned about my family and friends who don't know about Jesus. But I don't know if I know enough to explain it all to them. Can you use me? And if so, what are the main things I need to know and say?

The Bible Says...

"So we are Christ's official messengers. It is as if God were making his appeal through us. Here is what Christ wants us to beg you to do. Come back to God!" (2 Corinthians 5:20, NIrV).

So What Does It Mean?

God has a great plan to change the world and bring everyone back to him. And it's you and me. There's no plan B. We're it.

Why would God choose to use us? First, because we have a real story to tell about how God has changed our lives. Perhaps you came to know Christ through another person. That person probably lived in a way that helped you believe that God was really real. Second, God uses us because God wants to bless us. There's nothing more exciting than having God work through us to touch another person's life. And it's at those times when we need God most, that we also experience his power the most.

So, what are the main points to get across to explain God's plan to someone else? Basically, the Bible says:

• *All have sinned.* Explain that everyone has sinned. We've all done wrong things and fallen short of God's standards and plan for our lives.

"Yes, all have sinned; all fall short of God's glorious ideal" (Romans 3:23, LB).

• *Sin separates us from God.* Because we've all sinned, we cannot have a relationship with God. Our sin separates us from God forever.

"For the wages of sin is death" (Romans 6:23a, LB).

• *God reached out to us.* Because God loves us so much, he came up with a plan. He made a way for us to be able to have a relationship with him. He knew we couldn't get there on our own.

"For God loved the world so much that he gave his only Son so that anyone who believes in him shall not perish but have eternal life" (John 3:16, LB).

• *All you need to do is to trust him.* We deserved to be punished for our sins. But Jesus, who didn't deserve punishment, was punished for us when he died on the cross. He came back to life. Now he gives new life to all who give their lives to him.

"Now God says he will accept and acquit us—declare us 'not guilty'—if we trust Jesus Christ to take away our sins. And we all can be saved in this same way, by coming to Christ, no matter who we are or what we have been like" (Romans 3:22, LB).

Knowing these basics can help you share your faith more confidently. But remember, your personal experiences with Christ are some of the most powerful things you can share. Above all, ask the Holy Spirit to lead you in what to say to another person. And when to say it. He will!

Making It Personal

Who was a key person in your coming to know Jesus Christ?

What are some of the things he or she did or said that made the biggest difference?

Write the name of one person with whom you believe God wants to use you to share this good news.

Pray

Dear Lord,
So many of my friends need you in their lives. Help me say and do the right things to bring them to you.

Write a prayer for the person whose name you wrote above. Ask God to prepare his or her heart. Ask God to give you an opportunity to share what he has done in your life.

Where Do I Go From Here?

Dear God...

I feel pumped. What's next?

The Bible Says...

"We have everything we need to live a life that pleases God. It was all given to us by God's own power, when we learned that he had invited us to share in his wonderful goodness.

"Do your best to improve your faith. You can do this by adding goodness, understanding, self-control, patience, devotion to God, concern for others, and love. If you keep growing in this way, it will show that what you know about our Lord Jesus Christ has made your lives useful and meaningful" (2 Peter 1:3, 5-8, CEV).

So What Does It Mean?

Congratulations! You've made it all the way through these thirty foundational truths for helping you along the Christian journey. You've learned some very important things. And you've gotten into the habit of spending time with the Lord every day (or almost every day). That's the way he speaks to us best. And that's what helps us to grow consistently.

Ask your pastor, youth pastor, or another trusted Christian friend for the name of a book or Bible study to begin next. In the meantime, go back to this book's Table of Contents. Choose a topic that would be helpful for you to read again today. Do the same tomorrow. Do this until you've found the right book to start next. Or you may want to go through this entire book one more time. You'll be surprised to see how much you've learned and changed. And there will likely be a whole new set of things God wants to teach you as you read it through again.

In addition, begin reading one or two chapters in the Bible every day. Start with the Gospel of John in the New Testament and just keep going from there to Acts, Romans, and on.

Always ask God to teach you before you begin to read. When you land on something that really speaks to your heart, stop there and think about it for a bit.

Try using a journal (it can be just a notebook). In it you can write down things God is speaking to you about as well as questions and prayer requests you have.

You're well on your way! Remember God's word to you, "No eye has seen, no ear has heard, no mind has conceived what God has prepared for those who love him" (1 Corinthians 2:9b, NIV).

Making It Personal

Think about these past thirty days of spending time with God. What's the most important thing you read, learned, or thought about?

What's your biggest prayer request for the next thirty days?

Pray

Dear God,

Thanks so much for all you've been doing in my life these past weeks. It's been more than I ever could have expected. I pray that in the weeks ahead I will grow all the more into who you created me to be!

Pray about the next steps you think God wants you to take. Write them here, along with your commitment to keep growing!